D1474205

The Triumph of Religion

preceded by

Discourse to Catholics

The Triumph of Religion

preceded by

Discourse to Catholics

Jacques Lacan

Translated by Bruce Fink

polity

First published in French as *Le Triomphe de la religion* © Éditions du Seuil, 2005

This English edition © Polity Press, 2013

Polity Press
65 Bridge Street
Cambridge CB2 1UR, UK

Polity Press
350 Main Street
Malden, MA 02148, USA

ISBN-13: 978-0-7456-5989-3

A catalogue record for this book is available from the British Library.

Typeset in 12.5 on 15 pt Adobe Garamond by
Servis Filmsetting Ltd, Stockport, Cheshire
Printed and bound by Clays Ltd, St Ives plc

The publisher has used its best endeavours to ensure that the URLs for external websites referred to in this book are correct and active at the time of going to press. However, the publisher has no responsibility for the websites and can make no guarantee that a site will remain live or that the content is or will remain appropriate.

Every effort has been made to trace all copyright holders, but if any have been inadvertently overlooked the publisher will be pleased to include any necessary credits in any subsequent reprint or edition.

For further information on Polity, visit our website: www.politybooks.com

Contents

Note by Jacques-Alain Miller   vii

Discourse to Catholics
  Lecture Announcement   3
  I.   Regarding Morality, Freud Has
       What it Takes   5
  II.   Can Psychoanalysis Constitute the
       Kind of Ethics Necessitated by our
       Times?   32

The Triumph of Religion
  I.   Governing, Educating, and
       Analyzing   55
  II.   The Anxiety of Scientists   59
  III. The Triumph of Religion   63

v

CONTENTS

IV.   Closing in on the Symptom   68
V.   The Word Brings Jouissance   73
VI.   Getting Used to the Real   76
VII. Not Philosophizing   80

Bibliographical Information   86

Translator's Notes   87

Note

The two papers included here come from Lacan's oral work. I have chosen the titles and established the text.

The "Discourse to Catholics" includes two lectures – given on 9 and 10 March, 1960, in Brussels, at the invitation of the Faculté Universitaire Saint-Louis – which were billed as "open to the public." Lacan refers to them in chapters 13 and 14 of Seminar VII, *The Ethics of Psychoanalysis*.

"The Triumph of Religion" comes from a press conference held in Rome on October 29, 1974, at the French Cultural Center, when Lacan was there for a conference. He was interviewed by Italian journalists.

Some bibliographical information can be found at the end of this volume.

Jacques-Alain Miller

Discourse to Catholics

Lecture Announcement

The perspective opened up by Freud regarding the unconscious determination of man's behavior has impacted almost the entire field of our culture. Will it shrink in analytic practice to the ideals of normalization, ideals whose widespread circulation will offer a curious spectacle? It is well known that Dr. Jacques Lacan puts the psychoanalytic community to the test with a teaching that is very demanding regarding the principles of its action. At the Seminar at which he has trained an elite corps of practitioners and that he has given for seven years in Prof. Jean Delay's department [at St. Anne Hospital], he has arrived this year at the topic of the moral consequences of Freudianism, believing that he needs to venture beyond the shelter of a false objectivism to present objectively the action to which he has devoted his life.

He feels that such a presentation will be of interest to the public, and all the more so in that psychoanalytic action is judged in the private realm. He thus takes the risk today of introducing an untrained audience to an aim that goes to its very heart. Whereas Dr. Jacques Lacan does not believe that one can abandon to religious people alone the set of dogmas on which the Christian precept of our morality is based, involving the primacy of love and awareness of the neighbor, we will perhaps be surprised to see that Freud articulates the question here at its true lofty level, going far beyond the biases that are imputed to him by a phenomenology that is often presumptuous in its criticism. Hence the subtitles Dr. Lacan has provided us with for the two lectures, he reserving the right to adapt them as he sees fit:

I.   Regarding Morality, Freud Has What it Takes
II.   Can Psychoanalysis Constitute the Kind of Ethics Necessitated by our Times?

Philosophers will perhaps learn here to rectify the traditional position of hedonism; men of feeling to limit their study of happiness; men of duty to reconsider the illusions of altruism; libertines – yes, even them – to recognize the voice of the Father in the commandments his Death left intact; and spiritual men to resituate the Thing around which desire's nostalgia revolves.

I. Regarding Ethics, Freud Has What it Takes

Ladies and Gentlemen,

When Canon Van Camp came to ask, with his typically refined courtesy, if I would speak at the Faculté Universitaire Saint-Louis about a topic related to my teaching, I found, by God, nothing simpler than to say I would speak on the same topic I had chosen for the academic year that was beginning – this was back in October – namely, the ethics of psychoanalysis.

I am recounting here the circumstances or conditions of my choice essentially in order to avoid a few misunderstandings. When one comes to a talk by a psychoanalyst, one generally expects to hear once again a defense of psychoanalysis, which is so disputed, or a few insights regarding its virtues that are obviously, in theory, as everyone knows, of a therapeutic nature. That is precisely what I will not provide this evening.

I thus find myself in the difficult position of basically having to lead you into the midst of what I have chosen to discuss this year with an audience that is necessarily better trained for this research than you can be – regardless of your attraction to the topic and the attention I can see on all of your faces – since those who attend my seminar have been doing so for about seven or eight years.

My teaching this year is thus focused explicitly on a theme that is generally avoided: the ethical impact of psychoanalysis, of the morals that psychoanalysis can suggest, presuppose, or contain, and of the step forward psychoanalysis would perhaps allow us to take – how audacious! – in the moral realm.

I

To be quite frank, the person before you entered psychoanalysis late enough to have tried before – upon my word, like anyone who has been trained or educated – to orient himself in the realm of ethics. To orient himself theoretically, I mean, if not also, perhaps, by God, through several experiences often referred to as those of youth.

Nevertheless, he has been involved in psychoanalysis long enough to be able to say that he will soon have spent half his life listening to lives that are told, that are confessed [*s'avouent*]. He listens. I listen. Regarding these lives that, for almost four septenaries, I have listened to as they are confessed to me, I am in no way qualified to weigh their worth. And one of the goals of the silence that constitutes the rule of my listening is precisely to silence love. I will thus not betray their trivial and unique secrets. But there is something to which I would like to attest.

In the position that I occupy, and where I hope to finish out the remainder of my days, is something that will remain palpitating after me, I believe, as a waste product in the place I will have occupied. What is involved is, so to speak, an innocent questioning, or even a scandal, that can be formulated more or less as follows.

How does it happen that these good and accommodating men or neighbors, every one of whom props up a certain knowledge or is propped up by it, who are thrown into this business – to which tradition has given various names, that of existence being the latest in philosophy – into this business of existence (and what is lame about it is, I will say, what remains most confirmed), let themselves go to the point of falling prey to captivation by the mirages by which their lives, wasting opportunity, allow their essence to escape, by which their passion is toyed with, and by which their being, in the best of cases, only attains the scant reality that is affirmed only insofar as it has never been anything but disappointed?

This is what my experience shows me. This is the question I bequeath regarding the subject of ethics, where I muster what for me, as a psychoanalyst, constitutes my passion.

Yes, I know that according to Hegel all that is real is rational. But I am one of those who think that the converse is not to be disparaged – that all that is rational is real. There is only one small problem with this: I see that most of those who are caught between the one and the other, the rational and the real, are unaware of their reassuring compatibility. Will I go so far as to say that those who reason are to blame? One of the most worrisome applications of this much talked-about converse is that what professors teach is real and has as such as many effects as any other real – interminable, indeterminable effects – even if their teaching is false. This gives me pause for thought.

Accompanying a patient's enthusiastic rush toward a bit of reality [*reél*], I begin skidding with him on what I will call the creed of stupidities about which it is difficult to say whether contemporary psychology is the model or the caricature. Namely, the ego, considered to be a function both of synthesis and of integration; consciousness considered to be the culmination of life; evolution considered to be the pathway by which the universe of consciousness comes into being; the categorical application of this postulate to the individual's psychological development; and the notion of behavior, which is applied in a unitary fashion in order to break every bit of dramatic tension in human life down to the most ridiculous degree. All of this camouflages the following: nothing in the concrete life of a single individual allows us to ground the idea that such a finality directs his life and could lead him – through the pathways of progressive self-consciousness undergirded by natural development – to harmony with himself as well as to approval from the world on which his happiness depends.

Not that I don't recognize the effectiveness of the jumble that concretizes – on the basis of collective successions of what finally seem to be corrective experiments – under the heading of modern psychology. One finds there light forms of suggestion, so to speak, that are not without effect, and that can lead to interesting applications in the field of conformity and even of social exploitation. The problem is that this register has no hold on an impotence that merely grows to the extent that we have ever more occasion to implement the said effects. Man is ever more impotent to meet up anew with his own desire, and this impotence can go so far that he loses its carnal triggering. Even when the latter remains available, this man no longer knows how to find the object of his desire and no longer encounters anything but unhappiness in his search, living in an anguish that progressively shrinks what one might call his chance to invent.

What happens here in the shadows was suddenly shed light on by Freud at the level of neurosis. Corresponding to the eruption of his discovery into the basement was the advent of a truth. The latter concerns desire.

2

Desire is no simple thing. It is neither elementary, nor animalistic, nor especially inferior. It is the result, composition, or complex of an entire articulation whose decisive character I attempted to demonstrate in the second to last term of my teaching, of what I say where I do not shut up – and perhaps at some point I should tell you why.

The decisive feature of desire is not simply that it is full of meaning or that it is archetypal. To give you a quick survey, I will say that desire does not represent an extension of the so-called psychology of understanding, or a return to a micro/macrocosmic naturalism, to an Ionian conception of knowledge, or the figurative reproduction of primal concrete experiences, as so-called genetic psychoanalysis puts it these days. This last arrives at a simplistic notion that confuses the progression by which a symptom comes into being with regression along the therapeutic pathway, leading to a sort of telescoping relationship that wraps itself around a stereotyped frustration in the relationship of dependency that ties a child to its mother.

All of that is but semblance and source of error. Desire – insofar as it appears in Freud's work as a new object for ethical reflection – must be resituated within the context of Freud's intentions.

The central characteristic of the Freudian unconscious is to be translatable, even where it cannot be translated – in other words, at a certain radical point of the symptom, namely the hysterical symptom, which is undeciphered by its very nature and thus decipherable – that is, [even] where the symptom is represented in the unconscious only by lending itself to the function of what can be translated.

What can be translated is what is technically called the signifier. It is an element that presents two dimensions: it is synchronically linked to a battery of other elements that can be substituted for it and it is available for diachronic use – that is, for the constitution of a signifying chain.

Indeed, there are in the unconscious signifying things that repeat and that constantly run unbeknown to the subject. This is similar to what I saw earlier today when I was coming to this room – namely, the advertisements running in streaming lights along billboards on the fronts of our buildings. What makes them interesting to clinicians is that, under the right conditions, they manage to insert themselves into what fundamentally has the same nature as them: our conscious discourse in the largest sense – namely, all that is rhetorical in our conduct, which is far more extensive than we think. I will now leave the dialectical side of things.

Here you will ask me what these signifying elements are. I will answer that the purest example of signifiers are letters, typographical letters.

You will tell me that letters have no meaning. This is not necessarily true. Consider Chinese letters. For each of them you find in the dictionary a range of meanings that in no wise pales in comparison with the range of meanings corresponding to our words. What does this mean? What do I mean by giving you this answer? Not what you might think, since it means that the definition of these Chinese letters, just like the definitions of our words, has a scope that consists merely in a collection of usages.

Strictly speaking, a meaning is born from a set of letters or words only insofar as it presents itself as a modification of their already received usage. This implies first that any [new] signification this set acquires draws on the significations to which it has already been linked, as foreign to one another as the realities involved in this reiteration may be. This is the dimension that I call metonymy, which makes poetry of all realism. This implies, on the other hand, that any new signification is generated only by the substitution of one signifier for another, which is the dimension of metaphor by which reality becomes infused with poetry. This is what happens at the level of the unconscious, making it such that the unconscious is by nature a discourse, assuming we allow ourselves to qualify a certain use of linguistic structures as a discourse.

Does poetry already operate at this level? Everything leads us to suspect as much. But let us confine ourselves to what we see. What we see are effects of rhetoric. Clinical work confirms this, for it shows us these effects creeping into concrete discourse and into everything that can be discerned regarding our behavior as marked by the stamp of the signifier. This will bring those of you who are somewhat informed back to the very origins of psychoanalysis: the interpretation of dreams, slips of the tongue, and even jokes. This will alert the others, those who are more advanced, to the direction in which an effort to increase our knowledge base is being made.

What, need we but read our desire in such hieroglyphs? No. Look back at the texts by Freud on the themes I just mentioned – dreams, slips of the tongue, and jokes – and you will never see desire being clearly articulated. Unconscious desire is what is meant by the one who or the thing that proffers unconscious discourse. This is why the latter speaks. Which means that he is not obliged, as unconscious as he may be, to speak the truth. Moreover, the very fact that he speaks makes it possible for him to lie.

Desire corresponds to the true intention of this discourse. But what can the intention of a discourse be in which the subject, insofar as he speaks, is excluded from consciousness? Here we have something that is going to pose a few totally new problems to the moral philosophy of good intentions, which our modern exegetes have apparently not yet decided to broach.

At least this is true of a Thomist who, quite some time ago already, found nothing better to do than to compare Freud's doctrine to the core of Pavlov's work in order to bring it to the distinguished attention of Catholics. Curiously enough, this brought him, beginning then, and even now, praise both from those he commented on – namely, the professors at the arts college that awarded his doctoral degree – and from those one can say he betrayed, that is, his psychoanalytic colleagues. I have too much esteem for the present literary and psychoanalytic capacities of my audience to think that their satisfaction with him is anything other than that of a complicit silence regarding the difficulties psychoanalysis truly brings into play in ethics. The starting point of reflection would, it seems, be to observe that perhaps the more a discourse is deprived of intention, the more it can be confused with truth, with *the* truth, with the very presence of truth in the real, in an impenetrable form.

Must we conclude from this that it is a truth to no one until it is deciphered? What are we to think of a desire with which consciousness no longer has anything to do except to know it to be as unknowable as the "thing in itself," but which is nevertheless recognized to be the structure of the "for itself" *par excellence* that a chain of discourse is? Doesn't Freud seem to you to be more applicable than our philosophical tradition as regards conducting oneself correctly in relation to this extremity of intimacy that is at the same time excluded internality?

It is excluded except perhaps here in Belgium, which has long been buffeted by the winds of mystical sects, not to mention heresies, in which this intimacy became an issue not so much of a political choice as of religious heresy, whose secret led to the characteristic effects of a conversion in people's lives, before persecution showed that it was dearer to them than their lives.

I am broaching here a remark that I don't think is out of place at the university where I am speaking.

The coexistence [at this university] of two separate streams of teaching – one that is denominational and one that is not – is no doubt progress, reflecting tolerance. It would be all the more ungracious of me to contest it in that we ourselves in France have quite recently taken a similar path. It seems to me, nevertheless, that this separateness leads to a sort of mimesis of powers that are represented in it, which results in what I will call a curious neutrality. It seems to me less important to know which power benefits from this neutrality than to be sure that in any case it is not detrimental to all those affected by these powers.

A sort of strange division in the field of truth has thus been propagated. I will say that, to me – and the very least one can say is that I profess no denominational affiliation – an epistle by St. Paul is as important to comment on in ethics as one by Seneca. But I wonder if both don't lose something essential to their message if they are not commented on in the same place.

In other words, to designate a realm as that of belief, inasmuch as it may be such, does not seem to me to suffice to exclude it from the examination of those who are attached to knowledge. Moreover, to those who believe, it is certainly a kind of knowledge [*un savoir*] that is at stake in it. St. Paul pauses to tell us:

> What shall we say then? *Is* the law sin? Certainly not! On the contrary, I would not have known sin except through the law. For I would not have known covetousness unless the law had said, "You shall not covet." But sin, taking opportunity by the commandment, produced in me all *manner of evil* desire. For apart from the law sin *was* dead. I was alive once without the law, but when the commandment came, sin revived and I died. And the commandment, which *was* to *bring* life, I found to *bring* death. For sin, taking occasion by the commandment, deceived me, and by it killed *me*. [Romans, 7:7–11]

It seems to me that it is not possible for anyone, whether a believer or a non-believer, not to find himself called upon to respond to what such a text implies by way of a message articulated regarding a mechanism that is, moreover, alive and well, perfectly perceptible and tangible to a psychoanalyst. To tell you the truth, when in one of my classes [in Seminar VII] I recited this text without any transition from my own remarks, my students only noticed that it was no longer me who was speaking [in my own name] because of its rhythm, the halftime that shifts music to another perceptible mode. Be that as it may, the shock they received from the story of this music proves to me that, whatever their background, it had never made them hear before the meaning of this text at the level at which I situated it in their practice.

There is a certain flippancy in the way science disposes of a field regarding which it is not clear how it can so easily lighten its load. Similarly, faith has, a bit too often for my taste, been letting science resolve problems when questions translate into suffering that is a bit too hard to handle.

I am certainly not going to complain about the fact that clergymen have been sending their flocks to psychoanalysts. They are certainly doing the right thing there. What jolts me a bit is that, when they do so, they stress, it seems to me, that the individuals they send are sick and can thus find some help in analysis, even if the source of the help is, let us say, a bad one.

If I am wounding a few people of good will, I hope that I will nevertheless be forgiven on Judgment Day owing to the fact that I will have, at the same time, encouraged this goodness to withdraw into itself – namely, regarding the principles of a certain non-will.

3

Everyone knows that Freud was a crude materialist. Why then wasn't he able to resolve the problem, which is nevertheless so easy, of moral agency [*instance*] by resorting, as is classic, to utilitarianism?

Such recourse ultimately involves behavioral habit, which is recommended for the well-being of the group. It is so simple and, moreover, it is true. The attraction of utility is irresistible, so much so that we see people damning themselves for the pleasure of giving their [modern] conveniences to other people who, they've got it into their heads, cannot live without their help.

This is undoubtedly one of the most curious phenomena of human sociability. But what is essential is the fact that the useful [*utile*] object incredibly leads to the idea of sharing it with the greatest number, because it is truly the need for the greatest number as such that gave them the idea [in the first place].

There is only one difficulty here, which is that, whatever the benefit of utility and the extension of its reign, it has nothing to do with morality. The latter consists primarily – as Freud saw and articulated, and he never changed his tune regarding it, unlike many classical moralists, or even traditionalists, or even socialists – in the frustration of a jouissance that is posited by an apparently greedy law.

Freud no doubt claims to rediscover the origin of this primordial law, using a Goethean method, by following traces of critical events that have remained perceptible. But don't be fooled: the ontogenesis that reproduces phylogenesis is merely a keyword used here in order to convince everyone. It is the *onto* [in ontogenesis] that serves here as a smokescreen [*trompe l'oeil*], for it is not the individual as an entity [*l'étant*] but rather the subject's relation to being, assuming this relation is based on discourse. The past of the concrete discourse of the human line can be refound therein, inasmuch as in the course of man's history things have happened to him that have changed the subject's relation to being. Thus, apart from the alternative – the hereditability of acquired traits that Freud seems to accept in certain passages – is the tradition of a condition which, in a certain way, grounds the subject in discourse.

I cannot fail to emphasize here the full import of a condition that I'm surprised no commentator has brought out: Freud's meditations on the function, role, and figure of the Name-of-the-Father, in addition to his entire ethical reference revolving around the properly Judeo-Christian tradition, to which they are thoroughly linked in his work.

Read the short book with which Freud's meditations end a few months before his death, but which had already been consuming and preoccupying him for many years: *Moses and Monotheism*. This book is merely the endpoint and fulfillment of what began with the creation of the Oedipus complex and continues in a book that is so poorly understood and so badly appraised: *Totem and Taboo*. In it you will see the figure that appears of the father concentrating upon itself love and hate;

it is a magnified, magnificent figure, marked with a style of active and suffered cruelty.

We could debate at length about what led Freud to this image, about the personal reasons that led him to it – namely, his family, his experience of childhood, his father, old Jacob Freud, prolific and hard-working patriarch of the small family from the indestructible race. But what is important is not to examine Freud's psychology.

There would be a lot to say on the topic. In my view, his psychology was more feminine than anything else. I see the trace of this in the extraordinary monogamistic requirement that led him so far as to submit to a kind of dependency that one of his disciples, the author of his biography [Ernest Jones], calls "uxorious." I can't really imagine Freud as a father in everyday life. I believe that he experienced the Oedipal drama only at the level of the analytic horde. He was, as Dante says somewhere, its *Mère Intelligence*.

As for what I myself have called the Freudian Thing, about which I will speak to you tomorrow evening, it is first of all Freud's Thing – namely, something that is diametrically opposed to intention–desire. What is important is for us to situate how Freud discovered this Thing and where he began from when he followed its trail in his patients.

Totem and Taboo revolves around the function of the phobic object, and it is this function that guided Freud toward the function of the Father. Indeed, this function constitutes a turning point between the preservation of desire in its omnipotence – and not, as people in a certain analytic tradition write, creating problems, the omnipotence of thought [i.e., "magical thinking"] – and the correlative principle of a prohibition that leads to the setting aside of this desire. The two principles wax and wane together even if their effects are different: the omnipotence of desire engenders fear of the defense that ensues in the subject, and prohibition drives the statement of desire away from the subject in order to transfer it to an Other, to the unconscious that knows nothing of what is propped up by its own enunciation.

What *Totem and Taboo* teaches us is that the father prohibits desire effectively only because he is dead and, I will add, because he does not know it himself – "it" here referring to the fact that he is dead. This is the myth that Freud proposes to modern man, insofar as modern man is the one for whom God is dead – in the sense that he believes he knows it.

Why does Freud adopt this paradoxical position? In order to explain that man's desire will be all the more threatening and thus that its prohibition will be all the more necessary and severe. God is dead, nothing is permitted anymore. The decline of the Oedipus complex is the mourning of the father, but it leaves us with a durable consequence: the identification known as the superego. The unloved father becomes the identification upon which one heaps reproaches in oneself. This is what Freud brings us, joining up through a thousand threads of his testimony with a very ancient myth, the one that makes the entire ruined Earth depend on something wounded, lost, or castrated in the mysterious King.

We must examine in detail what this scrutiny of the function of the Father represents and introduce here the most precise distinctions, especially between what I have called the symbolic instance – the father who promulgates, who is the seat of the articulated law in which is situated the waste product of deviation or deficit around which the structure of neurosis is specified – and, on the other hand, something that contemporary analysis constantly neglects even though it is perceptible and alive everywhere for Freud: namely, the impact of the real father. Even when this impact is good or beneficial, it can, as a function of this structure, lead to ravaging and even maleficent effects.

There is considerable clinically articulated detail that I cannot go into or guide you into here if only because of the limited time available to us. Suffice it to say that, if there is something that Freud situates at the forefront of ethical experience, it is the drama that is played out in a certain place that we must certainly recognize – regardless of Freud's justified denial of having any personal penchant for religious sentiment or religiosity – as that in which an experience is articulated as such that Freud doesn't even bother to qualify as religious, since he tends to universalize it. He nevertheless articulates it using the very terms with which characteristically Judeo-Christian religious experience has itself historically developed and articulated it.

In what sense does monotheism concern Freud? He knows, as well as one of his disciples does, that the gods are innumerable and changing like the figures of desire, that they are living metaphors. But this is not the case for the only God. If Freud seeks out the prototype thereof in a historical model, the visible model of the Sun, from the first Egyptian religious revolution, that of Akhenaten, it is in order to link back up with the spiritual model of his own tradition: the God of the Ten Commandments.

He seems to adopt the first by making Moses into an Egyptian in order to repudiate what I will call the racial root of the phenomenon, the psychology of the Thing. The second makes him articulate as such in his account the primacy of the invisible, insofar as it characterizes the promoting of the paternal bond, founded on faith and law, taking precedence over the maternal bond, which is founded on a manifest carnality. These are Freud's terms.

The sublimable value of the Father's function is underscored directly at the same time as the properly verbal or even poetic form of its consequence surfaces, since it is to the tradition of the prophets that Freud attributes responsibility for making the monotheism that was repressed by a more formalist sacerdotal tradition progressively resurface in the history of Israel, through the ages. With an image, and following Scripture, this return basically paves the way for a possible repetition of the attack on the primal Father in the drama of redemption, where this attack becomes blatant – I'm still summarizing what Freud wrote here.

If I highlight these essential features of Freudian theory, it is because, compared to what it represents by way of courage, attention, and confronting the true question, it seems to me of slight importance to fault Freud for not believing that God exists or even for believing that God does not exist. The drama in question is articulated with universal human value. In scope, Freud here assuredly goes beyond the framework of all ethics, at least of those ethical systems that intend not to proceed through the pathways of the Imitation of Christ.

Will I say that Freud's pathway proceeds at man's level? I would not say so willingly. You shall perhaps see tomorrow where I intend to situate Freud in relation to the humanist tradition.

At the point at which we find ourselves in relation to the latter, I see man overdetermined by a *logos* that is found wherever one also finds his *Ananke*, his necessity. This *logos* is not a superstructure. Indeed, it is rather a substructure, since it undergirds intention, articulates the lack of being in man, and conditions his life of passion and sacrifice.

No, Freud's thought is not humanistic. Nothing allows us to apply this term to him. His thought is nevertheless tolerant and tempered. Let us call it humanitarian, despite the nasty overtones this word has acquired in our times. But, curiously enough, his thought is not progressive – it has faith neither in the movement of immanent freedom, nor in consciousness, nor in the masses. And it is in this respect, strangely enough, that Freud goes beyond the bourgeois milieu of ethics against which he could not, moreover, rise up, no more than against everything that is occurring in our era, including the ethics that reigns in the East and which, like any other, is an ethics of moral order and service of the State.

Freud's thinking is altogether different from this. Pain itself seems useless to him. Discontent with civilization comes down to this, in his view: so much pain for a result whose final structures are rather aggravating. The best people are those who always require more of themselves. Let us grant a few moments of repose to the masses as well as to the elite.

Amidst such an implacable dialectic, isn't this a derisory palinode? I hope to show you tomorrow that it is not.

Morality, as the ancient Greek tradition teaches us, has three levels: the sovereign good, honesty, and utility.

As regards the sovereign good, Freud's position is that pleasure is not it. Nor is it what morality refuses. Freud indicates that the good does not exist and that the sovereign good cannot be represented.

It is not Freud's intent to turn psychoanalysis into some kind of outline of honesty for our times. He is far from Jung and his religiosity, which one is astonished to see preferred in Catholic milieus, and even Protestant ones, as if pagan gnosis or even rustic witchcraft could renew the pathways to the Eternal.

Let us remember that Freud is the one who taught us that guilt finds its roots at the unconscious level, where it is linked to a fundamental crime for which no one can individually answer, nor has to. The reason for guilt nevertheless lies at the deepest level of man, once desire is the scale of articulated language even if it is not articulable.

You will no doubt stop me here. Reason – what are you saying? Can there be logic where there is no negation? Certainly, Freud said and showed that there was no negation in the unconscious, but it is also true, when one analyzes the topic rigorously, that negation stems from the unconscious. This is nicely highlighted in French by the articulation of the discordant "*ne*" that no necessity of the statement absolutely necessitates. "*Je crains qu'il ne vienne*" means I am afraid he is coming, but also implies to what extent I desire it. Freud speaks assuredly at the heart of the knot [*noeud*, which in French sounds just like *ne*, not] of truth where desire and its rule go hand in hand, in this "it" [or "id"] whereby desire's nature partakes less of the entity [*l'étant*] of man than of the want-to-be whose mark he bears.

I hope to show you that Freud – without pedantry or the reformer's zeal, and open to a folly [*folie* also means madness] that goes far beyond its roots as sounded by Erasmus – indicates to us the agreement between man and nature, which mysteriously opposes itself, and where he would like to find a way to get a respite from his pain, finding reason's measured time.

II. Can Psychoanalysis Constitute the Kind of Ethics Necessitated by our Times?

Monseigneur, Ladies, and Gentlemen,

I left you last night with a series of roughly hewn judgments regarding Freud, his position in ethics, and the honesty of his aim.

I believe that Freud is far closer than he allows to the Christian commandment "Love thy neighbor as thyself." He does not allow it; he repudiates it for being excessive as an imperative, if not for being mocked as a precept by its apparent fruits in a society that nonetheless calls itself Christian. But it is a fact that he investigates the point.

He speaks about it in a surprising text entitled *Civilization and its Discontents.* His whole discussion revolves around the meaning of the "as thyself" at the end of the formulation. The mistrustful passion of he who unmasks makes Freud pause before this "as." The weight of love is at stake. Freud knows in effect that self-love is great; he knows it better than anyone, having recognized that delusions are powerful because they find their source therein. "*Sie lieben also den Wahn wie sich selbst*" – they love their delusions as themselves, he wrote. This power is the one he designated with the name "narcissism." It involves a secret dialectic in which psychoanalysts have a hard time finding their way around. It is in order to allow us to conceptualize it that I introduced into psychoanalytic theory the strictly methodological distinction between the symbolic, the imaginary, and the real. Here's how it goes:

I undoubtedly love myself, and with all the persistent passion in which life's bubble seethes and swells in a palpitation that is both voracious and precarious, not without fomenting in its bosom the sore point from which its unity will spring forth anew, disseminated by its very shattering. In other words, I am tied to my body by the characteristic energy that Freud placed at the core of psychical energy: the Eros which makes living bodies come together to reproduce, which he calls libido.

But what I love, insofar as there is an ego to which I am attached with a mental concupiscence, is not the body whose beating and pulsation are all too evidently beyond my control, but an image that misleads me by showing me my body in its *Gestalt*, its form. It is beautiful, big, and strong – it is all the more so inasmuch as I am ugly, small, and pitiful. I love myself insofar as I essentially misrecognize myself – I merely love an other, an other [*autre*] with a lowercase initial *o*, hence my students' use of the term "little other."

There is nothing surprising in the fact that it is myself alone that I love in my semblable. Not merely in neurotic devotion, if I indicate what psychoanalytic practice teaches us, but also in the broad, widespread form of altruism, whether educative or familial, philanthropic, totalitarian or liberal, to which people would often wish to see the magnificent croup of the unfortunate beast respond with a sort of vibration – man transfers nothing but his self-love [*amour-propre*]. This love has indubitably been long since detected in its extravagances, even glorious ones, by moralists as they investigated its supposed virtues. But psychoanalytic investigation of the ego allows us to identify it with the form of the goatskin bottle [*outre*], with the outrageousness of the shadow whose prey the hunter becomes, and with the emptiness [*vanité*] of the visual form. This is the ethical face of what I have articulated, in order to convey it, with the term "mirror stage."

As Freud teaches us, the ego is made up of

identifications that are superimposed like [layers of] peels, constituting a sort of wardrobe whose items bear the mark of being ready made, even if the way they are put together is often bizarre. Owing to identifications with his imaginary forms, man believes he recognizes the core of his unity in the guise of self-mastery by which he is necessarily duped, whether it is illusory or not, for this image of himself in no way contains him. If it is immobile, only his grimaces, flexibility, disarticulation, dismemberment, and scattering to the four winds begin to indicate what his place in the world is. And yet it took a long time for him to abandon the idea that the world was created in his image and for him to recognize that what he rediscovered by way of this image – in the form of signifiers which his industriousness had begun to strew throughout the world – was the essence of this world.

We see here the decisive importance of the discourse of the so-called physical sciences and of something that raises the question of an ethics which can measure up to an era like ours.

What scientific discourse unmasks is that nothing any longer remains of a transcendental aesthetic by which harmony would be established, even if that harmony were [now] lost, between our intuitions and the world. No analogy can henceforth be established between physical reality and any sort of universal man. Physical reality is fully and totally inhuman. The problem that arises for us is no longer that of the *co-naissance* [a play on *connaissance*, knowledge, and *naissance*, birth] or of a co-naturalness by which the affinities of appearances open up before us. We know what's what on earth and in heaven – neither contains God – and the question is what we make appear there in the disjunctions constituted by our technology [*techniques*].

Our technology, I say, and you will perhaps correct me on this point: "Human technology that serves man." Of course, but it has taken on a measure of effectiveness inasmuch as its crux is a science that was unleashed, as it were, only by giving up all anthropomorphism, even that of the fine *Gestalt* of spheres whose perfection was the guarantee that they were eternal and, moreover, that of the force whose impetus was felt at the heart of human action.

Our science is a science of little signs and equations. It partakes of the inconceivable, insofar as it takes Newton to be right where Descartes was wrong. It is no accident that this science takes on an atomic form, for it is structured by the production of the atomism of the signifier. People wished to reconstruct psychology upon this atomism, but we protested against it when it came to understanding ourselves: we did not recognize that we were inhabited by this atomism. This is why Freud begins with the hypotheses of psychological atomism, whether or not we can say that he fully endorses them. He treats the elements of association not as ideas which must be purified by experience, but as signifiers whose constitution implies first their relation to what is hidden that is radical in structure as such, that is, the crux of permutation – namely, that one thing can be put in the place of another thing and that it can represent the other thing solely in this way.

The meaning of the word "representation" is entirely different here than it is in painting: *Anschauung*, where reality [*réel*] is supposed to engage in some sort of striptease with us. Moreover, Freud articulates it properly – not using the term *Vorstellung* [(re)presentation], although the accent is placed on the representative in the material of the unconscious – using instead *Vorstellungsrepräsentanz* to say what is repressed.

I won't go into any detail here. I'm not slipping into some sort of philosophical construction; I am trying to find my way in the most immediate material of my experience. If I refer to Freud's work to attest to this experience, it is because we find in it a rare conjunction – despite the negative appraisal of critics who are just as trifling as they are lacking in understanding, which happens to those who have but the word "understanding" on their lips – a rare concordance, as I was saying, exceptional in the history of thought, between Freud's speaking [*dire*] and the Thing he discovers for us. What this involves by way of lucidity on his part goes without saying, but, after all, in accordance with what he discovers for us, I will go so far as to say that the accent of consciousness placed on one or another point of his thought is secondary here.

In his work, representations are no longer even remotely Apollonian. They have an elementary destination. Our neurological apparatus operates in such a way that we hallucinate what may answer in us to our needs. This is perhaps an improvement compared to what we can presume about the reaction mode of an oyster attached to its rock, but it is dangerous in that it places us at the mercy of a simple taste-related or percussive sampling, so to speak, of sensation. In the final analysis, we need but pinch ourselves to know if we aren't dreaming. Such is at least the schema that we can provide of what is articulated in the twofold principle that commands the psyche, according to Freud: the pleasure principle and the reality principle, inasmuch as the physiology of man's so-called natural relationship to the world is articulated in them.

I won't dwell on the paradox constituted by such a conception from the standpoint of a theory of behavioral adaptation, inasmuch as the latter is ruled by the attempt to reconstruct a certain conception of ethology. We must see what is introduced, in this schema of the [psychical] apparatus, by its effective functioning insofar as Freud discovers therein the chain of strictly unconscious effects.

People have not authentically perceived the reversal that the unconscious brings with it at the very level of the twofold principle: a reversal or, rather, a challenging of the elements with which these principles are ordinarily associated.

The function of the reality principle is to concern itself with the satisfaction of need, and particularly what is episodically attached to it by way of consciousness, insofar as consciousness is tied to the elements of the privileged sense [i.e., sight] in that they involve the primordial narcissistic image. Conversely, thought processes, all the thought processes – including [*compris*], I almost said compromising, judgment itself – are dominated by the pleasure principle. Situated in the unconscious, they are drawn out of it only by theorizing verbalization that extracts them for reflection. The sole principle of their effectiveness for this reflection is the fact that they are already organized, as I said yesterday, according to the structure of language.

The true reason for the unconscious is that man knows at the origin that he subsists in a relationship of ignorance, which means that man's psyche involves a first division by which everything with which he resonates – regardless of the heading under which it is placed, whether appetite, sympathy, or in general pleasure – leaves out and skirts the Thing to which everything he experiences, in an orientation of the already predicative signifier, is destined.

I did not [have to] unearth all of that in the *Entwurf*, the "Project for a Scientific Psychology," discovered in the papers that make up Freud's correspondence with Fliess. It is quite clear there, but it only takes on value by showing the skeletal outlines of a reflection that blossomed into an indisputable practice. The tight link Freud demonstrates between what he calls *Wissbegierde*, which in German is very strong, *cupido sciendi* – in French we would have to say "curious avidity" – and the decisive turning of the libido is a sweeping fact whose repercussions are seen in a thousand determining features in any individual child's development.

Nevertheless, this Thing is no object and could not be one, in that its end [*terme*] arises as a correlate of a hypothetical subject only insofar as this subject disappears or vanishes – the subject fades but does not end – beneath the signifying structure. Indeed, what intention shows is that this structure is already there before the subject begins to speak and makes himself into the bearer through speech of any truth whatsoever, before he lays claim to any recognition whatsoever. The Thing is thus that which – in any living being that discourse comes to inhabit and that offers itself up in speech – marks the place where he suffers from the fact that language manifests itself in the world. In this way, being appears everywhere that the Eros of life encounters the limit of its unitive impulse [*tendance*].

This impulse toward union is, in Freud's work, at an organismic or biological level, as they say. Nevertheless, it has nothing to do with what is apprehended by biology, the newest of the physical sciences. It is a mode of eroticized capturing of the body's principal orifices. Hence the famous Freudian definition of sexuality, from which people wanted to deduce a supposed "object relation" said to be oral, anal, or genital. This notion of object relations harbors within itself a profound ambiguity, if not a pure and simple confusion, for it gives a natural correlate a characteristic of value that is camouflaged behind reference to a developmental norm.

It is with such confusions that [Christ's] malediction regarding those who "bind heavy burdens, hard to bear, and lay them on men's shoulders," found in Matthew [23:4], will strike those who authorize in man the presupposition of some personal shortcoming [*tare*] at the core of dissatisfaction.

While Freud detected the reasons for debasement in the sphere of love better than ontological casuistry did over the course of centuries, he related it first to the Oedipal drama – in other words, to a dramatic conflict articulating a more profound splitting of the subject, an *Urverdrängung*, that is, an archaic repression. Thus, even as he left room for secondary repression that forces the currents he calls tenderness and desire to go their separate ways, Freud still never had the audacity to propose a radical cure for a conflict that was structural in nature. If he outlined, as no primitive or modern typology of character has ever done, what he designated as libidinal types, it was expressly in order to formulate that he had gotten to the point of confirming that there was undoubtedly, in the end, something irremediably awry in human sexuality.

This is undoubtedly why Ernest Jones – in the obituary that it devolved on him to write for his most passionately admired master – could not help but situate Freud, owing to his conception of man's destiny, under the patronage, he writes, of the Church Fathers, even though Freud was the declared partisan of a resolutely antireligious *Aufklärung* [Enlightenment].

Let us go further. Although Freud holds sexual morality responsible for the nervousness pervasive in modern civilized man, he never claims to have a general solution to propose regarding a better way to configure this morality.

The object recently imagined by psychoanalysis as a measure of one's libidinal correspondence [with reality] would inform with its standard a whole reality as the mode of the subject's relation to the world: a voracious relation, a retentive relation, or – as people express themselves using a term that bears the mark of a moralizing intention about which one must say that the defenders of psychoanalysis in France thought they had to embellish its first manifestation – an "oblative" [altruistic or self-sacrificial] relation that would signal the idyllic advent of the genital relationship. Alas, is it up to the psychoanalyst to repress the fundamental perverseness of human desire into the hell of the pre-genital because it is connoted with affective regression? Is it up to him to make us forget the truth revealed in the ancient mysteries that "Eros is a black God"?

The object in question merely traces out a crude condemnation of the effects of frustration that analysis takes it upon itself to temper. The

sole result is to camouflage the far more complex sequences, whose richness and singularity
alike seem to be strangely eclipsed in a certain
orthopedic utilization of analysis.

The singular – I am searching here for a French
equivalent of the English term "odd" – role of the
phallus in the fundamental disparity of its function, the virile function, is situated in the two
ways of surmounting the Other's castration. Its
dialectic [in masculinity] seems to have to involve
the formulation "He is not without having it,"
whereas femininity is subject to an early experience of deprivation in order to wind up wishing
to make the phallus *be* symbolically in the product of childbirth, whether this product turns out
to have it or not.

This third object, the phallus, detached from
the Osirian dispersion to which I alluded earlier, serves the most secret metonymic function
depending on whether it intervenes in or is reab-
sorbed by desire's fantasy. By which I mean that
this fantasy is at the level of the unconscious
chain, which corresponds to the identification of
the subject who speaks as an ego in conscious discourse. In fantasy, the subject experiences himself
as what he wants at the level of the Other, this

time with an uppercase O – in other words, in the place where he is truth without consciousness and without recourse. It is here that he creates himself in the thick absence called desire.

Desire has no object, if not, as its singularities show, the accidental one, whether it is normal or not, that happens to manage to signify, whether in a flash or in a permanent relationship, the confines of the Thing – in other words, of this nothing around which all human passion tightens its spasm with a shorter or longer modulation and a periodic return.

The passion of the mouth that is most passionately stuffed is for the nothing by which, in anorexia, it demands the [kind of] deprivation that reflects love. The passion of the miser is for the nothing, to which the object enclosed in his beloved treasure chest is reduced. How could man's passion manage to find satisfaction without the copula that joins being as lack with this nothing?

This is why, whereas a woman may be secretly content deep down with the person who satisfies both her need and this lack, a man, seeking his want-to-be beyond his need – which is nevertheless so much better assured than a woman's – is inclined toward inconstancy, or, more exactly, toward a duplicating of the object, whose affinities with what there is by way of fetishism in homosexuality have been very curiously explored in analytic practice, if not always correctly and well put together in psychoanalytic theory.

But do not believe, nonetheless, that I think women are more favored when it comes to jouissance. Their difficulties are hardly in short supply and are probably more profound. But it is not my objective here to go into that, even though our group will soon be taking it up in collaboration with the Dutch Society of Psychoanalysis.

Have I at least succeeded in conveying to you the topological chains that situate at the heart of each of us the gaping place from which the nothing questions us about our sex and our existence? This is the place where we have to love the neighbor as ourselves, because in him this place is the same.

Assuredly, nothing is closer to us than this place. To express it, I will borrow the voice of the poet who, regardless of his religious accents, was recognized by the Surrealists to be one of their elders. The poet in question is Germain Nouveau, the one who signed himself *Humilis*.

Frère, ô doux mendiant qui chantes en plein vent,
Aime-toi, comme l'air du ciel aime le vent.

Frère, poussant les bœufs dans les mottes de terre,
Aime-toi, comme aux champs la glèbe aime la terre.

Frère, qui fais le vin du sang des raisins d'or,
Aime-toi, comme un cep aime ses grappes d'or.

Frère, qui fais le pain, croûte dorée et mie,
Aime-toi, comme au four la croûte aime la mie.

Frère, qui fais l'habit, joyeux tisseur de drap,
Aime-toi, comme en lui la laine aime le drap.

Frère, dont le bateau fend l'azur vert des vagues,
Aime-toi, comme en mer les flots aiment les vagues.

Frère, joueur de luth, gai marieur de sons,
Aime-toi, comme on sent la corde aimer les sons.

Mais en Dieu, Frère, sache aimer comme toi-même
Ton frère, et, quel qu'il soit, qu'il soit comme toi-même.

[Brother, oh sweet beggar who sings in the wind,
Love thyself, as heaven's air loves the wind.

Brother, driving the oxen through the clods of earth,
Love thyself, as in the fields the glebe loves the
earth.

Brother, who makes blood-red wine from golden
grapes,
Love thyself, as the vine loves its golden clusters.

Brother, who bakes bread, golden outside and fair
inside,
Love thyself, as in the oven the outside loves the
inside.

Brother, who makes cloth, joyous weaver of fabric,
Love thyself, as in itself the wool loves the fabric.

Brother, whose boat hews the blue-green waves,
Love thyself, as at sea the deep loves the waves.

Brother, lute player, gaily marrying sounds,
Love thyself, as one senses the string loves the
sounds.

But in God, Brother, know how to love thy brother
As thyself, and whatever he may be, let him be as
thyself.]

Such is the commandment of love for one's neighbor.

Freud is right to stop short there, dumbfounded by its invocation, because psychoanalytic practice shows – and analysis articulates as a decisive discovery – the ambivalence by which hatred follows like a shadow all love for the neighbor who is also what is most foreign to us.

How then not to plague him with tests designed to get him to make the only cry that could allow us to know him? How is it that Kant does not see what his thoroughly bourgeois practical reason runs up against when it is set up as a universal rule? The debility of the proofs he gives for it has only human weakness going for it, which sustains the naked body that Sade gives it: boundless jouissance for all. It would take more than sadism – an absolute love, in other words, an impossible one.

Isn't this the key to the function of sublimation that I am currently getting those who attend my Seminar to dwell upon? Man tries to compromise with the Thing in various forms: in the fundamental art that makes him represent it in the hollow in the vase in which the longstanding alliance is grounded; in religion which inspires in him fear of the Thing and makes him stay at the proper distance from it; and in science, which does not believe in it, but which we now see confronted with the fundamental wickedness of the Thing.

Trieb [drive], a primary and eminently enigmatic notion in Freud's theory, tripped over the form and formulation of the death instinct, scandalizing his disciples. The death instinct is, nevertheless, the response of the Thing when we don't want to know anything about it. It doesn't know anything about us either.

But isn't this also a form of sublimation around which man's being, once again, turns on its hinges? Isn't libido – about which Freud tells us that no force in man is more readily sublimated – the last fruit of sublimation with which modern man responds to his solitude?

Let prudence keep me from moving ahead too quickly!

May the laws, by sole means of which we can find anew the path of the Thing, be guarded by us. They are the laws of speech by which the Thing is surrounded.

I have raised before you the question that is at

the very heart of Freud's practice. Perhaps I have done so madly, for the pitfalls of psychological mastery are hardly revealed even to those who might appear to be most able to avoid them.

I have gone so far as to say that there have been classes in which we discussed Christ's psychology. What does that mean? Is it in order to know in what way his desire could be grasped?

I teach something whose endpoint is obscure. I must apologize here – I was led to it by a pressing necessity of which the one that brought me here before you is but a small moment, which will help you, I hope, to understand.

But I am not happy to be here [*être là*]. This is not my place, which is by the bedside of the patient who speaks to me.

Thus let not the philosopher stand up, as happened to Ibn Arabi, to greet me overflowing with signs of his consideration and friendship, to end up embracing me and saying, "Yes."

Of course, like Ibn Arabi, I would respond by saying "Yes" to him. And his joy would be heightened when he observed that I had understood him.

But, realizing what incited his joy, I would have to add, "No."

The Triumph of Religion

I. Governing, Educating, and Analyzing

Why do you say that the psychoanalyst's position is an untenable one?

I have commented that I am not the first to have said so. Someone we can trust regarding the analyst's position – namely, Freud – said so.

Freud extended the fact of being untenable to a number of other positions, including that of governing. Which is already to say that an untenable position is precisely what everyone rushes toward, since there is never any lack of candidates running for office. The same is true of psychoanalysis, where we encounter no dearth of candidates.

"Analyzing," "governing," and Freud added "educating."

Candidates are even less scarce in this last arena. It is a position that is even reputed to be advantageous. I mean that, not only are candidates in no way lacking, but there is no shortage of people who receive the stamp of approval – that is, who are authorized to educate. This does not mean they have the slightest idea what is involved in educating. People don't perceive very clearly what they are wanting to do when they educate. They try nevertheless to have some smidgeon of an idea, but they rarely reflect about it.

The sign that there is nevertheless something that can worry them, at least from time to time, is that they are occasionally taken with something very specific, that analysts alone know very well – namely, anxiety. They become gripped with anxiety when they think about what it is to educate. There are tons of remedies for that anxiety, in particular a certain number of "conceptions of man," conceptions of human nature. These conceptions of human nature vary quite widely, although no one seems to notice.

I just recently became interested in a very fine book related to education, in a series edited by Jean Château who was a student of Alain's. I haven't even finished it yet. It is absolutely sensational. It begins with Plato and continues by discussing a certain number of pedagogues. One perceives in reading it that at the root of education there lies a certain idea of what one must do to create men – as if it were education that did so.

But, frankly, it isn't necessary to educate man. He gets his education all by himself. In one way or another, he educates himself. He must learn something, and that requires a little elbow grease. Educators are people who think they can help him. They even consider that there is a minimum to be furnished in order for men to be men and that this requires education. They are not at all wrong. Indeed, a certain amount of education is necessary in order for men to manage to stand each other.

In comparison to that, there is the analyst.

Governing and educating are quite different from analyzing in that they have been going on since time immemorial. And they are everywhere: governing and educating never stop. The analyst, on the other hand, has no tradition. He is a total newcomer. Thus, among the impossible positions, a new one happened to arise. Few analysts are especially comfortable occupying this position, given that we have but one short century behind us to help us get our bearings. The novelty of it reinforces the impossible nature of it.

Analysts, starting with the first of them, had to discover this position, and they very clearly realized its impossible nature. They extended it to the position of governing and educating. As they are merely at the stage of awakening, it allowed them to perceive that people who govern and educate haven't, in the final analysis, the foggiest idea what they are doing. Which does not stop them from doing it, and even from doing a halfway decent job. Governors are needed, after all, and governors govern – that's a fact. Not only do they govern, but everyone is glad they do so.

So we come back to Plato.

Yes, we come back to Plato. It is pretty easy to come back to Plato. Plato said a huge number of banalities and naturally we return to them.

The arrival of the analyst at his proper function allowed us to cast a glancing light on what the other functions are. I devoted a whole year of my seminar to explaining the relationship that springs from the fact of the existence of this completely new function which is the analytic function, and to explaining in what respect it sheds light on the others [Seminar XVII, *The Other Side of Psychoanalysis*]. This led me to show which links they do not have in common. If they had them in common, they would not differ. I showed how that could be handled in a very simple manner thanks to four little elements that change places and revolve. This gives rise to some very interesting things.

II.   The Anxiety of Scientists

There is something Freud didn't talk about because it was taboo to him – namely, the scientist's position. It too is an impossible position, but science does not yet have the slightest inkling that it is, which is lucky for science. Scientists are only now beginning to have anxiety attacks.

Their anxiety attacks are no more important than any other such attacks. Anxiety is something that is altogether hollow [*futile*] and worthless [*foireuse*]. But it is amusing that recently we have seen certain scientists working in entirely serious laboratories suddenly becoming alarmed, having livers [*avoir les foies*] – which signifies in French having the heebie-jeebies, and saying to themselves: "Suppose that someday, after we have truly made a sublimely destructive tool with all these little bacteria with which we are doing such marvelous things, someone takes them out of the laboratory."

It hasn't happened yet. They haven't gotten

that far. But they have begun to get the idea that they could create bacteria that would be resistant to everything, that would be unstoppable. That would clear the surface of the globe of all the shitty things, human in particular, that inhabit it. And then they suddenly felt overcome with pangs of responsibility. They put an embargo on a certain number of experiments.

Perhaps it is not such a bad idea; perhaps what they are doing could be very dangerous. I don't believe so. The animal world is indestructible. Bacteria won't get rid of all of that for us. But the scientists had a typical anxiety attack, and a sort of prohibition, at least provisional, was announced. They told themselves that they must think twice before going further with certain experiments involving bacteria. What a sublime relief it would be nonetheless if we suddenly had to deal with a true blight, a blight that came from the hands of the biologists. That would be a true triumph. It would mean that humanity would truly have achieved something – its own destruction. It would be a true sign of the superiority of one being over all the others. Not only its own destruction, but the destruction of the entire living world. That would truly be the sign that man is capable of something. But it gets them quaking a bit in their boots, all the same. We aren't there yet.

Since science hasn't the foggiest idea what it is doing, apart from having a little anxiety attack, it will go on for a while. Because of Freud, probably, no one has even dreamt of saying that it is just as impossible to have a science that produces results as it is to govern or educate. But if we can nevertheless have a slight suspicion of that, it is thanks to analysis.

Analysis is an even more impossible profession than the others. I don't know if you are aware of this, but psychoanalysis is concerned especially with what doesn't work. Because of this, it concerns itself with what we must call by its name – I must say that I am still the only one who has called it by this name – the real.

The real is the difference between what works and what doesn't work. What works is the world. The real is what doesn't work. The world goes on, it goes round – that's its function as a world. To perceive that there is no such thing as a world – namely, that there are things that only imbeciles believe to be in the world – it suffices to note that there are things that make it such that the world [*monde*] is revolting [*immonde*], so to speak. This is what analysts deal with, such that, despite what one may think, they are confronted with the real far more than even scientists are. Analysts deal with nothing but that. They are forced to submit to it – that is, to brace themselves all the time. To do so, they must have awfully good armor to protect them from anxiety. The very fact that they can at least speak about anxiety is quite something.

When I spoke about anxiety some time back, in 1962–3, at the moment at which in French psychoanalysis – or whatever it is that goes by that name – the second split occurred, it had a bit of an effect, it created quite a maelstrom. One student of mine, who had attended the whole of my year-long seminar on anxiety [Seminar X], came to see me all enthusiastic, so much so that he said that he had to put me in a bag and drown me. He loved me so much that this seemed to him the only possible conclusion. I hurled insults at him and threw him out. That didn't stop him from surviving or even from finally joining my institute [the École Freudienne de Paris].

You see how things are. Funny things [*drôler-ies*] happen. This is perhaps the pathway by which one can hope for a future for psychoanalysis – psychoanalysis would have to devote itself sufficiently to funny things.

III.   The Triumph of Religion

You said earlier that, "If religion triumphs, it will mean that psychoanalysis has failed." Do you think that people now go to a psychoanalyst like they used to go to their confessor?

I guess someone had to ask that question. This confession business is preposterous. Why do you think people confess?

When you go to your analyst, you confess too.

Absolutely not! They are not at all alike. In analysis, we begin by explaining to people that they are not there in order to confess. It is the first step of the art. They are there to talk – to talk about anything.

How do you explain the triumph of religion over psychoanalysis?

Religion does not triumph by means of confession. If psychoanalysis won't triumph over religion it is because religion is invincible. Psychoanalysis will not triumph – either it will survive or it won't.

You are convinced that religion will triumph?

Yes. It will triumph not only over psychoanalysis but over lots of other things too. We can't even begin to imagine how powerful religion is.

I spoke a moment ago about the real. If science works at it, the real will expand and religion will thereby have still more reasons to soothe people's hearts. Science is new and it will introduce all kinds of distressing things into each person's life. Religion, above all the true religion, is resourceful in ways we cannot even begin to suspect. One need but see for the time being how the place is crawling with it. It's absolutely fabulous.

It took some time, but they [Christians] suddenly realized the windfall science was bringing them. Somebody is going to have to give meaning to all the distressing things science is going to introduce. And they know quite a bit about meaning. They can give meaning to absolutely anything whatsoever. A meaning to human life, for example. They are trained to do that. Since the beginning, religion has been all about giving meaning to things that previously were natural. It is not because things are going to become less natural, thanks to the real, that people will stop secreting meaning for all that. Religion is going to give meaning to the oddest experiments, the very ones that scientists themselves are just beginning to become anxious about. Religion will find colorful [*truculent*] meaning for those. We need but look at how it is working now, how they are becoming abreast of things.

Will psychoanalysis become a religion?

Psychoanalysis? No. At least I hope not.

Perhaps it will in fact become a religion – who knows, why not? – but I don't think that is my way. Psychoanalysis did not arise at just any old historical moment. It arose correlative to a major step, to a certain step forward made by scientific discourse.

I will tell you what I say about it in my little paper, the one I thought up for this congress: psychoanalysis is a symptom. But we have to understand what it is a symptom of. It is clearly part of the discontents of civilization Freud spoke about. What is most likely is that people won't confine themselves to perceiving that the symptom is what is most real. People are going to secrete as much meaning as anyone could possibly wish for, and that will nourish not only the true religion but a pile of false ones too.

What do you mean by "the true religion"?

The true religion is the Roman one. To try to put all religions in the same basket and do what is called "the history of religions" is truly awful. There is *one* true religion and that is the Christian religion. The question is simply whether this truth will stand up – namely, if it will be able to secrete meaning to such an extent that we will truly drown in it. It will manage to do so, that's certain, because it is resourceful. There are already plenty of things that have been prepared for that. It will interpret the Revelation of St. John. There are already quite a few people who have tried their hand at it. It will find correspondences between everything and everything else. That's its very function.

The analyst is something else altogether. He is in a moment of molting. For a little while, people were able to perceive what the intrusion of the real is. The analyst remains there. He is there as a symptom. He can only last as a symptom. But you will see that humanity will be cured of psychoanalysis. By drowning the symptom in meaning, in religious meaning naturally, people will manage to repress it.

Are you following me? Has a little light bulb gone on in your head? Doesn't my position seem quite measured?

I'm listening.

Yes, you are listening. But are you catching hold of a little something that resembles the real?

I'm listening, I'm taking notes, and it's up to me, afterwards, to synthesize.

You're going to synthesize? Boy, are you lucky. Indeed, draw out of this whatever you can. A short-lived flash of truth has come from psychoanalysis – it won't necessarily last.

IV. Closing in on the Symptom

Your Écrits *are very obscure and difficult. Someone who wants to figure out his own problems by reading them is left profoundly unsettled. I have the impression that the return to Freud is problematic, for your return to Freud's texts renders the reading of Freud still more complicated.*

This is perhaps because I point out what Freud himself spent a long time drumming into his contemporaries' heads. *The Interpretation of Dreams* did not sell very well when it was first published, maybe 300 copies in 15 years. Freud had to work very hard to introduce his contemporaries to something as specific and yet as unphilosophical as the unconscious. Just because he borrowed the word *Unbewusste* from I forget whom – [Johann Friedrich] Herbart – doesn't mean it had anything to do with what the philosophers called "unconscious." There was no connection between them.

I have striven to demonstrate how Freud's unconscious is specified. Academics had little by little managed to digest what Freud had striven, very deftly, moreover, to make comestible, edible to them. Freud himself invited misunderstanding because he wished to convince people. The meaning of my return to Freud is to demonstrate what is incisive in what he discovered and what he put into play in a completely unexpected way, for it was truly the first time people were confronted with something that had nothing whatsoever to do with what anyone else had said before. The Freudian unconscious is the impact of something that is completely new.

Let me tell you something now about my *Écrits*.

I did not write them in order for people to understand them, I wrote them in order for people to read them. Which is not even remotely the same thing. It is a fact that, as opposed to what happened to Freud, there are quite a few people who read my *Écrits*. They certainly have more readers than Freud had for 15 years. In the end, of course, Freud had enormous success in selling his books, but it took a long time. I didn't have to wait nearly so long. It was a total surprise to me that my *Écrits* sold. I never understood how that happened.

What I have noticed, however, is that, even if people don't understand my *Écrits*, the latter do something to people. I have often observed this. People don't understand anything, that is perfectly true, for a while, but the writings do something to them. And this is why I would be inclined to believe that – as opposed to what one imagines when one peers in from the outside – people do read them. One imagines that people buy my *Écrits* but never open them. That is false. They open them and they even work on them. They even wear themselves out working on them. Obviously, when one begins my *Écrits*, the best thing one can do is to try to understand them. And since one does not understand them, one keeps trying. I didn't deliberately try to make them such that people don't understand them – that was a consequence of circumstance. I spoke, I gave classes that were very coherent and comprehensible, but, as I turned them into articles only once a year, that led to writings which, compared to the mass of things I had said, were incredibly concentrated and that must be placed in water, like Japanese flowers, in order to unfold. The comparison is worth whatever it's worth.

A long time back I already happened to write that it was often the case that one of the articles in my *Écrits* would become transparent after ten years. Even you, my dear sir, would understand. In ten years, my *Écrits*, even in Italy, even translated as they are, will strike you as small potatoes, as commonplace. For there is something that is rather odd, which is that even very serious writing eventually becomes commonplace. In very short order, you will see, you will encounter Lacan on every corner. Just like Freud! Everyone imagines he has read Freud because Freud is everywhere, in the newspapers, etc. That will happen to me too, you'll see, as could be the case for everyone if people got down to it, if people closed in a bit systematically on an altogether precise point which is what I call the symptom – namely, what isn't going well.

There was a moment in history at which there were enough people at loose ends to deal quite specifically with what wasn't going well and to provide a formulation of this "what isn't going well" *in statu nascendi*, as it were. As I explained earlier, all that will go round again, it will all be drowned in the same things, the most disgusting things we have seen in centuries, and which will naturally be re-established.

Religion is designed for that, to cure men – in

other words, so that they do not perceive what is not going well. There was a little flash – between two worlds, so to speak, between the bygone world and the world that is going to be reorganized as a superb world to come. I don't think that psychoanalysis holds any key whatsoever to the future. But it will have been a privileged moment in which one will have had a fair dose of what in my discourse I call the speaking being [*parlêtre*].

The speaking being is a term I use for the unconscious. The altogether unexpected and totally inexplicable fact that man is a speaking animal – to know what that is and with what this activity of speech is fabricated – is what I will try to shed some light on in my talk at the upcoming congress. It is closely linked to certain things Freud took up as related to sexuality. They are in fact related, but they are linked to sexuality in a very specific way.

There you have it. You'll see. Keep this little book in your pocket and reread it in four or five years – you'll see that it will have you licking your chops.

V. The Word Brings Jouissance

According to what I have understood, in Lacanian theory, at the basis of man there is not biology or physiology but rather language. St. John had already said: "In the beginning was the Word." You have added nothing to that.

I have added a little something to it.

"In the beginning was the Word," I couldn't agree more [John 1:1]. But, before the beginning, where was it? That's what is truly impenetrable. There is the Gospel according to John, but there is another thingamabob known as Genesis that is not altogether unrelated to the Word. People have jammed the two together by saying that the Word was the business of God the Father and that we recognize that Genesis was just as true as the Gospel according to John by the fact that it was with the Word that God created the world. It's a funny thingamajig.

In Jewish Scripture, Holy Scripture, it is quite clear what purpose is served by the fact that the Word was there not at the beginning but before the beginning. It is that, since it was before the beginning, God feels he has the right to make all kinds of reprimands to people to whom he has given a little gift, of the "little, little, little" sort, like one gives chickens. He taught Adam to name things. He didn't give him the Word, for that would have been too big a deal. He taught him how to name. It is no big deal to name, it is altogether within human ken. Human beings ask for nothing more than that the lights be turned down. Light in itself is absolutely unbearable. Moreover, no one ever talked about light in the century of the Enlightenment; instead they talked about *Aufklärung*. "Bring me a small lamp, I beg you." That's already a lot. It's already more than we can bear.

I am in favor of John and his "In the beginning was the Word," but it is an enigmatic beginning. It means the following: for the average Joe – for this carnal being, this repugnant personage – the drama begins only when the Word is involved, when it is incarnated, as the true religion says. It is when the Word is incarnated that things really start going badly. Man is no longer at all happy, he no longer resembles at all a little dog who wags his tail or a nice monkey who masturbates. He no longer resembles anything. He is ravaged by the Word.

I too think that it is the beginning. You tell

me I have discovered nothing. It's true. I have never claimed to have discovered anything. All the things I've taken up are things that I have cobbled together with a bit of this and a bit of that.

Now, above all, you can imagine that I have a certain amount of experience in this sordid profession known as being an analyst. I learned quite a bit there, and this "In the beginning was the Word" takes on more weight for me. I will tell you something: if there were no Word – which, it must be said, brings jouissance to all these people who come to see me – why would they come back if it weren't to treat themselves to a slice of the Word each time? I see it from that angle. It gives them pleasure, they rejoice in it. Without that, why would I have clients, why would they come back so regularly for years on end? Can you imagine that!

For analysis at least, it is true, in the beginning is the Word. If that weren't the case, I can't see what the hell we would be doing together.

VI. Getting Used to the Real

If human relations have become so problematic because the real is so invasive, aggressive, and haunting, shouldn't we . . .

The real we have thus far is nothing compared to what we cannot even imagine, precisely because the defining characteristic of the real is that one cannot imagine it.

Shouldn't we, on the contrary, deliver man from reality [réel]? Then psychoanalysis would have no further reason for being.

If reality [*réel*] becomes sufficiently aggressive . . .

The only possible salvation when faced with this reality [réel] that has become so destructive is to get away from it.

Completely push away reality [*réel*]?

A collective schizophrenia, in some sense. Hence the end of the role of psychoanalysis.

That is a pessimistic way of representing what I believe to be more simply the triumph of the true religion. To label true religion a collective schizophrenia is a highly peculiar point of view. Defendable, I admit, but very psychiatric.

It is not my point of view. I didn't mention religion.

No, you didn't, but I find that your words coincide astonishingly with what I started with – namely, that religion could, in the final analysis, very well fix all that. One must not over-dramatize, all the same. We must be able to get used to the real.

The symptom is not yet truly the real. It is the way the real manifests itself at our level as living beings. As living beings, we are eaten away at, bitten [*mordus*] by the symptom. We are ill, that's all. The speaking being is a sick animal. "In the beginning was the Word" says the same thing.

But the real real, as it were, the true real, is the one we can gain access to by a very precise pathway: the scientific pathway. It is the pathway of little equations. This real is precisely the one that is completely missing. We are altogether separated from it. Why? Because of something we will never get to the bottom of. At least I don't think so, even though I have never been able to demonstrate it absolutely. We will never get to the bottom of the relationship between speaking beings that we sexuate [*sexuons*] as male and the speaking beings we sexuate as woman. Here we get into a serious muddle. This is even what specifies what we call human beings. Regarding this point, there is no chance that it will ever succeed – in other words, that we will have the formula, something that can be scientifically written. Hence the proliferation of symptoms, because everything is linked to this. This is why Freud was right to speak of what he called sexuality. Let me put it like this: for the speaking being, sexuality is hopeless.

But the real to which we gain access with little formulas, the true real, is something else altogether. Up until now, all we have gotten from it are gadgets. We send a rocket to the moon, we have television, and so on. It eats us up, but it eats us up by means of things that it stirs up in us. It is no accident that television devours us. It is because it interests us all the same. It interests us by a certain number of altogether elementary things that one could enumerate, that one could make a short list of. The point is that we let ourselves be eaten. This is why I am not among the alarmists or among the anxious. Once we have had all we can take of them, we will stop and turn our attention to the true things – namely, what I call religion.

[. . .] The real is transcendent [. . .]. Our gadgets do, in fact, devour us.

Yes. But, personally speaking, I am not very pessimistic. There will be a tapering off of gadgets. Your extrapolation, making the real and the transcendent converge, strikes me as an act of faith.

What isn't an act of faith [foi]*, I ask you?*

That's what is horrible, it's always bedlam [*foire*].

I said "foi," I didn't say "foire."

It's my way of translating *foi. Foi* is a *foire*. There are so many faiths, faiths that hide in the corners that, in spite of it all, it can only be well said in the forum – in other words, at a fair.

THE TRIUMPH OF RELIGION

"Faith," "forum," "fair" – this is just a bunch of plays on words.

They are plays on words, that's true. But I attach a great deal of importance to plays on words, as you know. They seem to me to be the key to psychoanalysis.

VII.   Not Philosophizing

In your philosophy . . .

I am not a philosopher, not in the least.

[In Italian:] An ontological, metaphysical notion of the real . . .

It is not at all ontological.

You borrow a Kantian notion of the real.

It is not even remotely Kantian. I make that quite clear. If there is a notion of the real, it is extremely complex and in that sense it is not graspable, not graspable in a way that would constitute a whole.

It would be an incredibly anticipatory notion to think that the real constitutes a whole. As long as we haven't verified it, I think we would do better to avoid saying that the real in any way whatsoever forms a whole.

I happened to come across a short article by Henri Poincaré regarding the evolution of laws. You surely haven't read it as it is out of print, something only bibliophiles can find. Émile Boutroux, who was a philosopher, raised the question whether it was unthinkable that laws themselves evolve. Poincaré, who was a mathematician, got all up in arms at the idea of such evolution, since what a scientist is seeking is precisely a law insofar as it does not evolve. It is exceedingly rare for a philosopher to be more intelligent than a mathematician, but here a philosopher just so happened to raise an important question. Why, in fact, wouldn't laws evolve when we conceive of the world as having evolved? Poincaré inflexibly maintains that the defining characteristic of a law is that, when it is Sunday, we can know not only what will happen on Monday and Tuesday, but in addition what happened on Saturday and Friday. But it is not at all clear to me why the real would not allow for a law that changes.

It's obvious that we get into a complete muddle here. As we are situated at a precise point in time, how can we say anything regarding a law which, according to Poincaré, would no longer be a law? But, after all, why not also think that maybe someday we will be able to know a little bit more about the real? – thanks again to calculations. Auguste Comte said that we would never know anything about the chemistry of the stars and yet, curiously enough, now we have a thingamajig called a spectroscope that teaches us very precise things regarding their chemical composition. Thus we must be wary – things get developed, thoroughfares open up that are completely insane, that we surely could not have imagined or in any way have foreseen. Things will perhaps be such that we will one day have a notion of the evolution of laws.

In any case, I don't see how that makes the real any more transcendent. It is a very difficult notion to handle, a notion that people have thus far approached only with extreme caution.

It is a philosophical problem.

It is a philosophical problem, that's true. There are, in fact, little domains where philosophy might still have something to say. Unfortunately, it is rather curious that philosophy shows so many signs of aging. Okay, Heidegger said two or three sensible things. But it has nevertheless been a very long time since philosophy has said anything that might interest everyone. Moreover, it never says anything that interests everyone. When it does say something, it says things that are of interest to two or three people. After that, it shifts to universities and then it's shot – there is no longer the slightest philosophy, even imaginable.

One of you quite gratuitously referred to me earlier as Kantian. I have written only one thing about Kant, which is my short paper entitled "Kant with Sade." To be quite frank, I make Kant into a flower of sadism [*fleur sadique*]. No one paid the slightest attention to that article. Some second-rate fellow commented on it somewhere, and I don't even know if his commentary was ever published. But no one has ever sent me any remarks on that article. It is true that I am incomprehensible.

Since we were talking about the real as transcendent, I cited in passing the "thing in itself," but I was not suggesting that you were a Kantian.

I strive to say things that tally with my experience as an analyst. This experience is rather slight.
An analyst's experience is never based on enough
people to allow him to make generalizations. I
attempt to determine what an analyst can learn
from, to sketch out what the function of the
analyst implies by way of a rigorous conceptual
apparatus, and to indicate the guardrail one must
hold onto so as not to overstep one's function as
an analyst. When one is an analyst, one is constantly tempted to skid, to slip, to let oneself slide
down the stairs on one's backside, which is, all
the same, not very dignified as regards the analyst's function. One must know how to remain
rigorous, in such a way as to intervene only in a
sober and preferably effective way. I try to spell
out the conditions required for analysis to be serious and effective. This may seem to cross over
into philosophical territory, but it doesn't in the
slightest.

I am not developing any sort of philosophy – I
even mistrust philosophizing like the plague. If I
speak about the real it's because it seems to me
to be a radical notion with which to tie [*nouer*]
something together in analysis, but it is not the
only notion. There is also what I call the symbolic

and what I call the imaginary. I hold onto those as the three little ropes that alone allow me to remain afloat. I also propose them to others, of course, to those who are willing to follow me – but they can follow plenty of other people who do not fail to offer them their help.

What surprises me the most is that I still have so many people standing beside me. I cannot say that I have done nothing to keep them there. But I am not holding onto them by their collars. I'm not afraid of people leaving. On the contrary, I am relieved when they leave. Yet I am grateful to those who remain for discussing things with me from time to time, which gives me the sense that my teaching is not completely superfluous, that I teach them something that stands them in good stead.

How awfully kind it has been of you to ask me so many questions.

Bibliographical Information

"Discourse to Catholics": mentioning in his seminar on March 23, 1960, the lectures he had just given in Brussels, Lacan designates them with the words "my discourse to Catholics" (Seminar VII [Paris: Seuil, 1986], p. 211). Two successive versions of them were published in the organ of the École de la Cause Freudienne in Belgium: *Quarto*, 6 (1982): 5–24, and *Quarto*, 50 (1992): 7–20.

"The Triumph of Religion": the title and the section headings were provided by Jacques-Alain Miller. A first version came out in the internal bulletin of the École Freudienne de Paris, *Les Lettres de l'École*, 16 (1975): 6–26.

Translator's Notes

I would like to thank Mark and Katharina Kroll-Fratoni, as well as Héloïse Fink for their kind assistance on this translation. All errors here are my own.

The numbers in parentheses refer to the page and paragraph number of the present English edition.

Discourse to Catholics

(8, 1)   André Breton introduced the term *peu de réalité* (scant reality) in his 1924 "Introduction au discours sur le peu de réalité"; see *Point du Jour* (Paris: Gallimard, 1970); in English, see "Introduction to the Discourse on the Paucity of Reality," in *Break of Day*, trans. Mark Polizzotti and Mary Ann Caws, Lincoln: University of Nebraska Press, 1999, pp. 3–20.

(9, 2)   There may be a reference to "corrective emotional experiences" in the phrase "corrective experiments."

(11, 2)   "The so-called psychology of understanding" is a reference to Jaspers.

(11, 2)   On "genetic psychoanalysis," see H. Hartmann and E. Kris, "The Genetic Approach in Psychoanalysis," *The Psychoanalytic Study of the Child*, vol. 1, New York: International Universities Press, 1945; see Lacan's comments on it in *Écrits: The First Complete Edition in English*, trans. B. Fink, H. Fink, and R. Grigg, New York and London: W. W. Norton, 2006, p. 599.

(23, 3)   *Mère Intelligence* seems, rather, to come from Paul Valéry's *Poésie*.

(25, 1)   Or "in the sense that he believes He knows it."

(25, 2)   "God is dead, nothing is permitted anymore" is an obvious reversal of the line attributed to Dostoevsky (and found not quite word for word in *The Brothers Karamazov*, Part 4, Book 11, chapter 4, "A Hymn and a Secret"): "If God is dead, all is permitted."

(25, 2)   The "ancient myth" may be that of Cronus and Uranus.

(32, 3)   "Sie lieben also den Wahn wie sich selbst": see Sigmund Freud, *Aus den Anfängen der Psychoanalyse 1887–1902: Briefe an W. Fliess*, London: Imago, 1950, p. 101. [Citation from Draft H corrected.] Rendered as "Thus they love their delusion as they love themselves," in *The Origins of Psycho-Analysis: Letters to Wilhelm Fliess, Drafts and Notes 1887–1902*, New York: Basic Books, 1954, p. 113. Cf. *The Seminar of Jacques Lacan, Book III, The Psychoses*, trans. R. Grigg, New York: Norton, 1993, p. 214.

(34, 2)   *Semblable* is often translated as "fellow man" or "counterpart," but in Lacan's usage it refers specifically to the mirroring of two imaginary others (*a* and *a'*) who *resemble* each other (or at least see themselves in each other). "Fellow man" corresponds well to the French *prochain*, points to man (not woman), the adult (not the child), and suggests fellowship, whereas in Lacan's work *semblable* evokes rivalry and jealousy first and foremost. "Counterpart" suggests parallel hierarchical structures within which the two people take on similar roles – that is, symbolic roles – as in "The Chief Financial Officer's counterpart in his company's foreign acquisition target was Mr. Juppé, the *Directeur financier.*" I have revived the somewhat obsolete English "semblable" found, for example, in *Hamlet*, Act V, scene II, line 124: "his semblable is his mirror; and who else would trace him, his umbrage, nothing more."

(34, 2) *Amour-propre* can be rendered as self-love, self-regard, self-esteem, vanity, or pride.

(34, 2) "The outrageousness of the shadow whose prey the hunter becomes": there is a likely allusion here to the French expression *lâcher la proie pour l'ombre*, meaning to give up what one already has to go chasing after shadows. *Vanité* can mean vanity, pride, futility, emptiness, hollowness, or uselessness.

(35, 1) *Pelure* ([layers of] peels) is also a slang term for clothes.

(36, 2) A likely reference to the Copernican (or, more accurately, Keplerian) revolution, which required giving up the idea that the heavens moved according to perfectly spherical motions, and Freud's revolution, taking consciousness out of the center of man's motivation.

(37, 2) *Anschauung*: the Seuil French version reads *Abschäumungen* (evoking scum or dregs), but this does not seem to make sense given the context. *Anschauung* is based on the verb *anschauen*, meaning "to look" or "to watch," and is used in artistic contexts. An earlier version of the text reads *Abschattung* (shading), although a better alternative in this context might be *Abschattierung*.

(38, 2) "Those who have but the word 'understanding' on their lips" is a likely reference to Karl Jaspers.

(41, 1) The "Project for a Scientific Psychology" (1895) can be found in the Standard Edition, vol. 1, and in *The Origins of Psychoanalysis*, ed. Marie Bonaparte, Anna Freud, and Ernst Kris, trans. Eric Mosbacher and James Strachey, New York: Basic Books, 1954.

(41, 1) *Wissbegierde* is often rendered in English as inquisitiveness or intellectual curiosity.

(41, 1) *Cupido sciendi* means curiosity, desire to know the why and how of things.

(42, 1) Lacan often uses *tendance* (tendency) instead of *pulsion* (drive), especially in his early work.

(44, 2) Regarding Eros as a "black God," see *Écrits*, Paris: Seuil, 1966, p. 607.

(45, 3) The "Osirian dispersion" may be a reference to the earlier mentioned dismemberment and scattering to the four winds. *Le fantasme du désir* (desire's fantasy) could also be rendered as "desire qua fantasy."

(46, 3) "The passion of the miser is for the nothing, to which the object enclosed in his beloved treasure chest is reduced." This sentence is an obvious reference to Molière's *The Miser*.

(47, 2) Lacan gave a paper entitled "Guiding Remarks

for a Convention on Female Sexuality" (found in *Écrits*, 1966) at the International Colloquium of Psychoanalysis which took place September 5–9, 1960, at the University of Amsterdam.

(49, 7)   The poem, entitled *Fraternité*, "Brotherhood," can be found in *Poèmes d'Humilis*, Paris: La Poétique, 1910.

(52, 5)   Ibn Arabi met the philosopher Averroes, giving him only yes and no answers.

The Triumph of Religion

(56, 3)   Lacan is perhaps referring to Olivier Reboul's *L'Élan humain ou l'Éducation selon Alain*, Paris: Vrin, 1974, with a preface by Jean Château, published in a series overseen by Jean Château. Alain was one of the pseudonyms of Émile-Auguste Chartier.

(56, 4)   *Il n'est pas forcé que l'homme soit éduqué* (rendered in the text as "it isn't necessary to educate man") is somewhat ambiguous here: Lacan might mean that there is no need to educate people (period, or because in any case they educate themselves), that it isn't clear that people are ever educated by others (they educate themselves instead), or even that it isn't clear that people are ever truly educated or cultured.

(59, 3)   Something that is *foireuse* fails miserably or is cowardly.

(63, 2)   The interviewers refer back occasionally to a few remarks Lacan made prior to the beginning of the interview proper, which are not included in the published edition.

(72, 3)   The "little book" is likely a reference to the small two-volume paperback edition of a selection of the papers in Lacan's *Écrits* published in the Points collection by Seuil in 1970 and 1971 as *Écrits I* and *Écrits II.*

(74, 1)   "A little gift, of the 'little, little, little' sort, like one gives chickens" is not too clear to me, since one might say *petit-petit-petit* in French to an animal (like a dog) to encourage it to come over and receive a treat. Hence Lacan might be referring to the encouragement given by God so that someone accepts one of His gifts or the extremely tiny nature of the gift given.

(76, 3)   Things get confusing here, since *le réel* means both reality and the real (as Lacan defines it). It is not clear which is intended at which point, nor is it clear whether the interviewers have any understanding of the Lacanian notion of the real.

(77, 4)   Reading *rongés* (eaten away at) for *rangés* (ordered, arranged). *Mordus* could also be rendered by smitten.

(78, 1)   In Lacan's terminology, to sexuate (*sexuer*) might be rendered as "to differentiate sexually"; see Seminar XX, where Lacan uses the adjective *sexué* (as in *êtres sexués*, meaning beings that have a sex, a sexual organ, or that are *differentiated* into male and female), and presents his "formulas of sexuation."

(79, 5)   *Foire*, which literally means "market" or "fair," as in a festival, also means "mayhem." An older meaning is diarrhea.